WAVE BOOKS / SEATTLE / NEW YORK

DOUGLAS KEARNEY

Published by Wave Books

www.wavepoetry.com

Copyright © 2021 by Douglas Kearney

Wave Books titles are distributed to the trade by

Consortium Book Sales and Distribution

Phone: 800-283-3572 / SAN 631-760X

Library of Congress Cataloging-in-Publication Data

Names: Kearney, Douglas, author.

Title: Sho / Douglas Kearney.

Description: First edition. | Seattle : Wave Books, [2021]

Identifiers: LCCN 2020038258 | ISBN 9781950268160 (hardcover)

ISBN 9781950268153 (paperback)

Subjects: LCGFT: Poetry.

Classification: LCC PS3611.E177 S56 2021 | DDC 811/.6—dc23

LC record available at https://lccn.loc.gov/2020038258

Designed by Crisis

Printed in the United States of America

9 8 7 6 5 4 3 2 1

First Edition

Wave Books 091

To Furman Kearney 1939–2017

and Dorothy Martin 1918–2020

SHO

I. COME BACK STRIKING WHAT'S ABOVE

Buck   3

Well   5

Property Values   6

Do the Backseat Jam!   9

Everyday (I Gets)   10

Black Flight   11

Sand Fire (or The Pool, 2016)—   12

. . . Fox!   14

Livestock   16

Promissorry Note   18

Dogged   19

Close   23

Borax   26

The Post-   27

Welter   32

Demonology   33

2. A NEGROCIOUS SHOW OF FEELS

Sho   45

Static   49

Do the Cruiseline-up Slowgrind-up!   50

Negroes Are a Fatsuit, ❤ Hollywood, USA   51

Just Wanna Be Like   52

Deformation   54

First, She Cuts the Stems   55

The Showdown   58

Having Drowned Our Lovers,   65

Do the Six-Foot Jump Down!   66

Eulogy for a Pair of Kicks   67

Eulogy for an Afro Pick   70

The Drifters After School   72

Fire   73

". . . say the sacred words"   77

Manesology   80

Acknowledgments & Notes   85

1

COME
BACK
STRIKING
WHAT'S
ABOVE

BUCK

Seems some want some body bodied into street sweet meat.

Come and go get it!

We may not fight it but you'd like us to, too. Tool cocked back to make a no-way way you kick yourself in us. Umber-husked, our dirty look a dirty talk, begging for the something strong in your dom palm what smokes after doing it.

You order us scream the shut up.

You ever never hanker for surrender, so the hard:
cuff rough or stick licks.

Such a hurry! Look:
don't sweat,
don't fret.

You've ever done this before—

just fudge we're not real,
too dark here to tell.

Let's role:

they were fondling for my piece and finger banging a cash-box peeped through
convenient ballistic glass and face-lumped assed-out lawned till they popped the
juice came out them once their cig resisted lunged shiv-ish fit to shoot shot while
the woofers woofed their thick trap beats,

you said. And:

wanted us   in buck so buck us good   we'll buck   up after by candlelight, flower
petals   and we shall   we shall   like fucking champs, we. Oh, you're some machine
ain't you just   all up in it so we got   to be down, up to here.

WELL

I can't reckon, so I shake my head
to a woolie of ears and shut eye continu
-um. But I come to what I must want to be
: a well.

       By *I* I mean to call *we*,
       by *we* mean *what's at the bottom*
       of what I want to be—but that's not just
       so.
Well, I could find myself
a mountaintop to get to, to *there* on. Would I
then rung down myself to that stood water,
to what's drowned down in *it*
       —by which I mean *us*

   us

      us

PROPERTY VALUES

I aspire to be a CVS: *Lord, I wanna be*
a drugstore inna my heart—.
       Or a nice NEIGHBORhood,
a rapless gas-up—
       *inna my heart—*a "legit" "ballot"—
I perspire all night at it.

That my sweat, alchemical—
of shit, makes gold? Factual.

       Consider spent plantation dirt,
       arena turf, recording booth—
what transmogrifies these
sans my properties?

       If it could it should it's been bottled?

Me, I transude this solvent
sun up to—
       you know when—
then turn up
as you know what.

When it come time for one-time
to calm or gun sunshine
through us been crying hues,
mustn't the copper figure:

"Were its heart full of mouthwash, haircare products,
and miscellaneous, cheap electronics,
I'd serve, protect—"

Lord, my escalators'd all descend
and all for sale would glisten!

DO THE BACKSEAT JAM!

Stop there fam and jump to the brand spanking
back again you know how it go throw your hands
in the air when the lights on maestro raise the baton
and swing till you feel it the beat what's taking over
the street to the club when I say you say *ow*
it thumps let me see those hands all the people
in the be quiet get down on the floor like you know
this'll be the sure shot hit sweat through your clothes
you oughta you gotta you better put your hands
get ready for the you ain't ready for you gonna
listen up just as easy as falling off a countdown
three do it till it's done to the two the ones in blue
show em what you said to do to zeroes in brown
to the back to the back now you right in the jam!

EVERYDAY (I GETS)

I play the stone
while old River tonguing me
could fret me to grit—
      naw, not fret:
but loves me up what they do
what they do on the regular.
      I'm a lover
when I'm fighting. Peaceful,
here-lately. When I cry, say:
he's having River's babies,
      and so.

On the regular, I tend them,
I tend to look mad as I find me
more sand now, but naw.
      I'm fitful
when I'm sleeping. Wakeful,
a minute. My ears wet
when I get up. Like drowning,
      though I've never.
All my dreams Chevrolet heavy.
This land would swallow me
      for one damn pearl.

BLACK FLIGHT

Came I was way out as it flies
but an easy green and skies
isn't it? My cul-de-end is a nice, though
it's like the knot I keep my knickers in
to *hey there* stay here. Damn right
I'd rather not not squat some pissy asphalt
plot not. Rather put-em-up where I got
to picket in self-defense? Not *no* but if so
then where'd I roost my hoodie
among cooing polyphony? A no-go a no-no unless
I'm turned me round. Awful's everywhere I was—
I couldn't see me there—only pinions.
I've eyefuls of my absence everywhere
I'm here I go. *Hey there* I caw now
and mow and mow and mow.

SAND FIRE (OR THE POOL, 2016)—

chlorine and smoke lit our eyes
since it was we swam while fire made
a boxer's ear of sky—

      sweet, let go the side:
      you'll be fine—you dove
your violet ring from deepest cool—

      let me worry—while my Karo blood,
slick guts: just how it is—

      know how far the burning by
how small those first responders fly
at soot-bruised afternoon's skin—

      my guts crack slick knuckles,
Metformin putting work in deep—

      your catch at "how'd it start?"—

      I've told you yellow weather lights the litter,
oil spatters, common saltwort—

      don't breathe outside for days—
copters ring around and spill
to slow the 'flower—

      you goggle water and what "fire's gonna" eat eat
         sweet yes o *though not ours this time* because—
      let me worry over burning, over
drowning, how molasses blood loiters,

how we go below what *just*

        happens—

    hold your breath and

deeper deeper till you

        daughter daughter, come up clutching

        what is under—

        come back striking

            what's above.

. . . *FOX!*

lies on the shoulder
by my drive to work.
I wondered first *hell*
is (ripped pelt, spine

Hey fox! more grains than bones)
that? Then *whoa* yo, see me
glad! They're my favorite!
Eyeing each commute

Hey "fox!" hope no one takes it
away. Pretty sure you're an (—F
o   x—) (they do! Live here!)
Still there? How's your

Hey fox! fall? Well,
mine: leaves down
our new block! Red and gold
line the sides of our street

Hey fox! full of shhhhhhh,
they pile, we stomp
and we kick, scuffle through

Hey fox! (had none of this stuff
in our desert, nope!)
While the fox's dull fur

Hey fox! tears away tumbling off,
knapweed, as I fly

Hey fox! past in all thirsty speed—

LIVESTOCK

We've places in our properties for them,
lots for growing them into lots more for us.

In the places, there, we can watch them,
our faces like hands having want.

We, beaten by a cooler outside, said
they got a coat kind-of-a-skin sewn up on their bodies
until we slip them out it to wear it on us
and so we are we, for we wear their skin for us.

In our stove-like imagination, they are a wad of living Crisco,
Crisco shut up in them until we cook it out them, them out it,
into a pan, a cut of them fried in it out a can and into
our mouths, ground inside our mouths turning us into we-
who-wear-wads-of-body-in-our-bodies, the wad's bodies
on our bodies and so we are we, for we cook to enjoy this insiding.

Times, we've agreements with us to think for them
what we want them to think our love is like,
so we spin answers out slashed mouths, snipped tongues,
the splatterings beaten out their bodies in our lots for growing
us out of them:

we say they may say we are *universes gashing Earth*

or say they may say we are *baboons long ago hardened into clothes on them*

or that by their impassive, brown livings we guarantee us
they *want* in our mouths, to be our coats, to tiptoe
their bodies through our imaginations, graceful and doting
as mothers sewn to cries.

No no no no no—our love is nothing but *goodbye*,
and how we only want to love it all and so

all of them.

PROMISSORRY NOTE

1,863 − 1,526 = BILLIONS. Remit it in paper to ransom us 'napped
from families' to captors'. How much we want from each other or is it *for*—

someone should pay for what someone shouldn't have paid for—
those do-lows done to you-know-who done got passed gum checks,
                                                    bum 'backs,
                                                    and lumped some.

Cuffee coffles choc-a-block with cast of star-starved night,
still we called to see the bright side of whoever's newest mooning. Say,

even if what beeze lacked is not cents, isn't not a Black fist
a handout made blunt?

DOGGED

for Amaud Jamaul Johnson

Was my strength?

〜

Here, where I stood prior, I stay together—
like a dog and what it's caught, thrashing.
Up this maw is meat, thus: *tear away tear away*; then *bone*, thus:
what's left what's left.
Body down, I'm low so to hunt myself out, be got.
True true, I taut me some tether.
True true, I won't get away this time.

〜

I was at myself good there.
I crouch over me, clatter some haunch,
chatter some jaws, slaver slaver!
Want to get the meat to eat, better thrash my head:
no no no.
And caught, I'm all: *yes yes yes.*
My body there and torn away.
Open as maw was, then red.

〜

Once bone's got in the maw, I go prostrate:
devoted and theoretic.

꩜

In a poached country, all *no no no yes yes yes*, besetting itself to sic
what's itself, what's not, I'm those,
though such a country won't see me save I song
a knell, I'm thus used to song—the maw maws
into my body, my body *o* out the maw, all:
ooooo—
what it is, what it isn't.
Dogged, hunting—I'm in the way of such a country.

꩜

Better thrash if I want to *tear away*
and don't I want—
Better go *no no no.*
O so hole and hole so maw, what maw gives body, what that body sing.
O cuff!
O cordon!
O camera!
How being placed take you.
And I was saying about myself that this is—
O—such a country!
Hunting, country's all: more! more!

꩜

It give, too.

I was given the maw in the way of this country,

the maw used to—like *tool*

or like *accustomed*,

like *was*?

I was, anyway, given the maw.

A new name to be called when I get called,

to tell me when to do.

Simple instructions, tricks.

The dog stay, person go.

The dog get the meat to be got.

Yes yes yes, used to *it*.

Dogged dogged dogged to that place for which some sigh.

Not singing just now, though *o*—

all up in this country, so *no*.

No no—

I was never another thing.

Or meat?

My—my—my—

I tear it away in the way of such a country.

What it is, isn't, my body/the maw open,

singing now:—*of thee*—

Done singing just now.

Even so, I'm song, used to.

What's left what's left but the maw set upon my body,

my body, placed, all maw,

o—

The hunt, I'm used to *it*.

Still, how my pulse double.

CLOSE

for my family

The funk, recall,
as most Black Shit
once was and is
sickness. Fool,
how much oogie
in your jeebie?
Our Black asses
been hunkered in
this house, this now
"transitional" hood,
we steal away where
some call "White Cliffs"—
Fool! how much mni
in your pa?
Baby girl's coughs
been wet, she's set
at trilling
what pops. We spit
out this kitchen
bags up of chicken
bones to rank bins
in the alley till
soup tints no bowls.

It smells *close*, says N
for *funky* sure
since winter's
steady eavesdropping,
greedy tom-peeping
for five months, near. Now
Ma's newest facial
tincture scents foodish
out our lone loo. Fool,
how much acai
in your argan?
What we can't eat
off love even out
brown hands done, thus
I'm gone to market.
Once, my son shadowed—
copped kale, potatoes,
milk, cereals—though
now he must stir in-
house in his blossom
of must there, where
we close. Minding my gap
twixt strained neighbors,
drilling what have I
touched? My hands stay on
ashes, ashes—fool,
how much Jergens
in your Palmer's?

Out the store, day
broke, to dank-ass home,
got them bleach wipes, yeah,
back-porched in the cut.
We keep some sickness
out.

BORAX

This mud smirch of amok, it's them isn't we?

"Ain't'n't responsible for" messes of mess—
we're who were rigged by what had happened was.

Ain't it:
        (a) tainting (b) a tainted (c)
           who taints?

We make to stay at dunging up dung-heaps while the undung ones
aren't they? I'm at saying whatever shit cross their mind.

Who's low-down and dirty in their clean version?
They mean to keep it scrubbed isn't we?
They keep our hands stained as their shine.

THE POST-

Pulled free my skin at its linchpin for-to-be post-,
at last I am pink meat sitting at the desktop
typing things to do with my obsolete wrap:

      (1) bungee jump from sturdy limbs of Southern trees
      (2) bundle it for laundering with jockey silks and handkerchiefs
      (3) double dutch with Harlemites on Malcolm X
      (4) trade it in for right-to-work at harbor-based auction blocks
      (5)
      (6)
      (7)
      (8)
      &c.
      &c.
      and also that.

"Have you seen my lustrous skin?"
I mistook what she stroked for Saran.
Her handbag yorkie tugged it down
shucked her hips like stripped bikinis.
Her pink beneath, she seemed not to notice,
was just as new as a white POTUS.

Wind lifts my old skin, strolls it tipsy down the street.
A black-and-white trawls the curb—sees—and flashes lights;
then remembers when we are and pulls off! My skin
is quite the pip! Lingering by shop glass without appetite.

America is different now, isn't it.
The circling birds are tracing hugs,
yes. They want us *all* inside? There,
a pink child flies my skin, a kite!
"Look mommy," they said and mommy did.
"See how high it can go?" mommy said.
America is so different now, yes!

How many can fit in one skin?
The pronoun for "citizens": *us* or *them*?
Skinless now, as I've become, the rich air
agitates the pink. Gone so far
cleaving skins to ticker tape. The winners?
A parade for *them* next, from *us* for sure.
Best collect the litter when all is FIN;
once marching ends, we'll need loft it again.

WELTER

In the U.S., news broke regarding the discovery of a mass grave of
Rohingya Muslims at a human trafficking camp the same day as
the first Mayweather-Pacquiao welterweight championship bout.

Sic on it, cameras: queasy-green lush rush canopy—tilt down: thick bamboo cover twine-
bound—tilt down: welter, dirt's got rags to gag up, hijab stuck in dun incisors—zoom in
and rack: what's that flesh there, bone there bindled in cured skin—presence: fowl traffic,
twittering pittas, bulbuls up-ruffed, hum flies, flies plump as beans, boon the snowy-
browed, rufous-chested singsong, jungle jangle—cut: their throats, rufous, that was
months and was that months ago, the camp boomed—boom: get the boomed shotgun
mic out the shot, clean—cut: there're too many damn birds, dirty—cut: we can't use
this—wrap: swelter, late, wait, later—fight woot fight's tonight woot of the century
tonight woot weight: welters

DEMONOLOGY

What it fiends to be "END," but claims hella outsets;
cants *ever was* from amnesia worksheds.

How it bickers it's luminance out tomb-ish bunkers.

How it cooks up its figments was cool ipso factos.

Why its lines in the soil, fingers dirty and piss?
Thirsty ear see itself in A, B conversations.

Shit it names itself "KEY," trumps locks up to worship.
After gutting the fish, jots: FISHES CAN'T SWIM.

Still it lies and it lies and it lies and it lies
through its teeth, on the job, down with dogs, and in wait.

When it cries and it laughs! Oh it flinches and points!
Keeps bits of it hates what it's hanged among branches.

Where its maps are all Xs, there its heart is a shovel,
brain and genitals, shovels—where its eyes: empty sacks.

I know *exorcize*—what first meant to *conjure*,
but drifted to later, *drive out* what was called.

Come here. Come here. Come here. Come here.

2

A

NEGROCIOUS

SHOW

OF

FEELS

SHO

(a torchon after Indigo Weller)

Some need some Body
or more to ape sweat
on some site. Bloody

purl or dirty spit
hocked up for to show
who gets eaten. Rig

Body up. Bough bow
to breeze a lazed jig
and sway to grig's good

fiddling. Pine-deep
dusk, a spot where stood
Body. Thus they clap

when I mount *banc'*, jig
up the lectern. Bow
to say, "it's all good,"

we, gathered, withstood
the bends of dives deep
er, darker. They clap

as I get down. Sweat
highlights my body,
how meats dyed bloody

look fresher for show
ing, I got deep, spit
out my mouth, a rig

id red rind. Bloody
melon. Ha! No sweat!
Joking! Nobody

knows the trouble. Rig
full o' Deus. "Sho
gwine fix dis mess." Spit

in tragedy's good
eye! "This one's called. . . ." Jig
ger gogglers then bow

housefully. They clap.
". . . be misundeeeerstooooood!"
Hang notes high or deep,

make my tongue a bow—
what's the gift?! My good
song vox? The gift?!?! Jig

gle nickels from deep
down my craw. They clap.
I'se so jolly! Stood

on that bank. Body
picked over, blood E
rato! Braxton's *sweat*

y brow syndrome®, spit
out a sax bell ~~wring~~
a negrocious show

of feels. Fa sho, sweat
equals work. Bloody
inkpot of Body,

I stay nib dipped, show
never run dry! Rig
orously, I spit

out stressed feet. Lines jig!
Ha ha ha ha!!!! good
one [that/I] is, bow

deep but not out. Stood,
shining, dim. They clap,
waves slapping hulls. *Deep*

don't mean *sunken*; *good*'s
not *yummy*, right?! Bow,
blanched with foam, jig-jigs.

"This one's called . . ."—they clap—
"'_ _ _ _ _ _ _ _ _ _ _ _ barrow.' So much dep
ends / upon / dead _ _ _ _ _ _ _"; stood,

I, on that bloody
rise of sweet Body;
there *you* is, too. Sweat

it, let's. They clap—"Rig
ht?" some ask, post. Spit
tle-lipped: I said: "Sho."

STATIC

If we're bass-ackward, pair of steps back's a progress.
Left-foot, peg-foot, here, a turnstile spiral into that ill quadrille,
to a tune that loops till it cuts we stay attuned. Laps,
straight-up. Time double-took the same-old boreal commute

to what? Holler at us, vecinos. Who "move along"? When there
is nothing to see here, we're there.
Some static jump off, our rootedness nukes tupper-worn memory
for to grub its neckbone knuckles.

We bent on gnawing though it does to def our hearts'
condition; steady knowing knowing recollection 'members hunches.
That ol' "soon" we mint a "been." We take it, once again,
from the bottom: a-four, a-three, a-to, ago.

DO THE CRUISELINE-UP

SLOWGRIND-UP!

Line up every body for the rockin
'n' rollin you all in the groove from the windows
to the walls hump that back bend them knees grind
in tight on the one you're with it down to the floor
in this funky-ass joint to dawn till dark
fall next on deck a new cut y'all ain't never heard
but the man on the wheel will make you move
that hot body from coast to coast who got
the most soul folk wanna hear y'all holler follow
these steps if you step you best not too fast
now too far naw too low might catch the blues
on the one and three dammit don't lose the rhythm
gonna bring that beat back know how my crew
and I do best believe gonna see y'all work it!

NEGROES ARE A FATSUIT,

♥ HOLLYWOOD, USA

Direction: zooms inflate their wideness in whatever rerun I've them. I glut the frame with their material: a too muchness. Their being there strains our capacity to. That clip where they're a larding of city innards? A plumped oleo'ing on Southern dirt numbles? It's a funny that's a nasty what I'd never. The ticket's you'll get your helping heaping of enough's enough. Shot's crammed tight to affect cackish fat, your slighted eyes slough negro faux goo. At wrap, the scene is keen on stripping free of their de trop detritus, sweating (see: slave), as it were, as it were—

JUST WANNA BE LIKE

Was Him, once fini, on the beams,
prior, He's hewer of thorntree.
Could stretch tilapia and ewer,
dole it for all to take and eat.

For real though came pulverized metacarpus, metatarsus.
Some time later and later, latex, prosthesis, squib hocus—
once was "Green Goblin" be/been as "Him," at these thens,
still ogles nipples on tape. Philistines boo/'buke/hiss.

On His knees, when back beneath peace trees after the Foe tongued
the hot fork down the holiest holy cochlea. This I, This I—

A he/"Him" rode with the devil, once. Mr. Mad Max directed,
            now take it up, now put it down, and bleed good.
And good! Bus loads
like the sandal loads
packed to see him as "Him"/Him
opening, unrestricted, and so graphically.

                              I was directed:
If the other actors believe you're the king . . .
so I belted

"alas, alas for you" as "Him," again,

again at the strain of my range.

. . . the audience will believe

the King dies every year—

again, again for you—but *who seeks*

to save shall lose, thus encore!

The concessions looks looted, like whose temple is this?!

Moneychangers boo/'buke/hiss.

This I knew, since clip-on ties, pipe-cleaner puppets, lamb getups,

riser set-ups by height. *Find your suffering in His*; thus directed, reel:

the stripped, sinewy model/icon of Him as "Him." Break a leg!

> Lights dim, music up, stained glass cut
>
> to blood lit for love, for craft.
>
> Suspend.
>
> Now here's where you're there then,
>
> and can smell the stocks' dung
>
> while that young gal's milk
>
> mills Flesh from the star, hung.

DEFORMATION

She got an existential dilemma so I call her "Big Booty."
I wrote the rose bout herself, violet mess she muse me
to a long sharp sword. Old girl's dimensions defy my pen.
She a fox with a donkey or her kitten's a monkey?
She exists all at me dilemmically having twerked
in my cogito. Shawty what you think, shawty what you

think?

She need her head right. Cause what I look like falling in bitch
with a love? Shit—a stick, a bone, a cutlet to a loin,
loin to a cutlet. All that. So I spit: you my main thing,
your chicken and eggs got my rooster up to crow and scratch.
Say, she got a big booty so I call her out. Her name,
I don't know, but I mean to put it on her.

FIRST, SHE CUTS THE STEMS

for Yona Harvey

Systems are the end of a rope
and the rope. Measure and border
between out, in. What desire's
entwined there.
          A, say, Black
woman cuts peaches down:
          A paring knife will
do the trick. Orchard to house:
          A booming taxonomic
doing.
      Systems are frictions
that flimflam as liquids. They abrade
skin. In some systems,
skins are tenor. Vehicles, elsewhere.
In, out?
          An abrasion lets.
Low knocking at
        a door
means   a *Master/Mister*?
Some doorways kind of clear
their throats. From over: *Bring them faster!*
      Systems are what you're

steady doing. Louvered shutters
let the light.

A metonym

for how out outside
or inside in? *Well?!*
Christ, gal, it's hot as hell!
Some windows kind of roll
their eyes. Cut azaleas smell
red as heat—

Systems are will.
Squealing wood, hinge?—*oil that!*
Gentle rattle,
slats atremble means:

a breeze in,
say,   a Master's/Mister's room.
Black wench! Clipped finches'
shrill in brass lattice.

A bowl of peaches
set down fast as—*Hurry up!*
The door swung clear—*said,*
something cold! A passage out
to   a corridor,
then   a kitchen. There's
a pitcher what
sweats out itself what was in it.
Some kitchens kind of slit
the skins. What was in
them come undone. Systems are—When the, say,

Black woman cut—a paring knife will
do—then dropped the stems: entangled,
jutting out the kitchen bin—. Some houses
kind of suck their teeth. The pitcher
she pours in a cup. Fluid.—*be so
stupid!* Finches, azaleas rendered pets,
décor for those for whom some systems
are maintained. *Lazy!* A paring knife. Will.
And what are you doing—Calls of finches,
the walls flinch.—*with that*—Red as.

The bowlful of peaches, pell-mell,
while the breeze's cooling sweetness—

THE SHOWDOWN

is guns given druthers of *meaning* or *being*.
The old town looks empty save for chattering

lace palling panes awaiting murder
to see. Saltpeter, all. Even the birds

dizzying down wash-pan dusk. Buzzards:
God's finger. Now, one gun desires

meaning—"this is for"—and sputters.
That's the gun what wins. The other?

There's God's index, carnal, wrecking
a sunken cheek. If the gun reckoned

what it was, would it speak? Could it
whisper, not meaning nothing by it

in this panoramic utterance of dust?
Round these parts, the rotten cusses

won't carry their own infants.
Their hands set at what they ain't.

To have been gun
at duel. To serve one

simply. To cry
out, then only

be judged by spans
of silence.

The cinematic gun kills
only acting out itself.

The cinematic gun a spook
mask, gibbous skin and fixed,

rubber fangs. For the cinematic gun,
discharging beyond magazine

capacity is bug-eyed. Bucking
but not kicking accuracy cock-

eyed is, for the cinematic gun, kind
of cooning. See the cinematic gun

take the gun-virgin's hand when
the murderous goon, searching,

rounds the debris where the gun-
virgin trembles. "Lawsy! Lawsy!" Goon

gushes curlicued corn syrup, dye.
See the gun-virgin drop the empty

cinematic gun's smoky barrel
floorward? When it lands, hear:

"I loves every creature everywhar."
As we cut, hear: "That's all!"

"... and how will your lead ball
express?" boomed Flint Pistol.

"I've fixed light, but no ball,"
zotted Laser Gun. Cool,

leveled, they nodded there,
over Old Field's still scars

as the blood and ashes
slurried in low places.

And if the gun abets the bullet:
magazined, chambered, let out—

thus, a projected sense of further
and further of farther

and farther. Until careened
or ricocheted. Till a silk-screened

T-shirt, dark face, a sunrise,
a sunset—the block's sawed-off days.

Walker, driver, further,
farther. Shopper, corner-

bystander. Automatic gun
near too fast to have been,

but not so fast
as to be meaningless.

Needful, omnivorous gun!
Farther and further. Certain

weather! All you desperate guns,
waiting to speak and then.

HAVING DROWNED

OUR LOVERS,

the waters, tumescent,
go honey. Soon come some
million wings quavering,
buffeting sun away.

DO THE SIX-FOOT JUMP DOWN!

Back with a dusty how we get it in
till the cut it loose just like mama done
it all the way live and direct you dead
on it like pops hit the floor to that old
gritty sound it's spinning and the party
get low people in the groove somebody
scream the rhythm rock till the lights go dark
can't feel the tempo better lay it back
easy when the horns blow you know the time
dig it then you gonna BREAKDOWN show them
what you got nobody still standing up
against the wall last call all y'all you peep
the beat fade to my peeps in black don't wave
your hands at the drop crisscross look alive!

EULOGY FOR A PAIR OF KICKS

Almighty Lord, give unto me two pair
of wings to hie them unto Thee on high!
Permit these worn gums take the sky.

❧

     O my soles!

Where'er your tread pressed
the rugged earth's crust,
there you bore me home.
Now, I walk bare and alone.

God have mercy,
let be blessed
what shod me,
now, unbound for rest.

     O my shoes!

Stony the roads you trodded!
Storied how woe you cardboarded!
Brown bustered tot you untied!
Pennies of loafs what you tithed!

Tween feets too grown you squooshed!
Scores of just do you clean swooshed!
Every little step you big buckled!
Grip of skip skips you fake chucked!
Flip of cheap flop you half flapped!
Slick winter slips you black tracked!

This cold morning, yea, your whole body laced up,
eyestay to eyestay for you to go
in there, your last box, o hollow shell-toe:
      Did you know, did you do,
      was you, was you
      made me feel
      10 feet tall?

      All day, I'd dream about seeming
      tougher by your leather upper,
            your rubber under.
      Always, you'd hold me in
            your suede sides,
            your fresh holey mesh,
            your canvas coke-white
            as Death's icy cheek—

I pray you make your way unknotted
up the plum, custom shelves
      of Heaven's luxe walk-in.

I pray you may remain mated
over Celestial telephone wire,
  my dank slum cherries.

You who made stardust of crack vial,
mushed the mutt-mess pile,
crushed Kool butts, left roaches snuffed,
and stutter-stepped Satan's scuffing hoof:

Is God has watched, has numbered your steps
as barefoot cherubim hovered and cheered:
  It's the—! The—! It's gotta be the—!

So, kick back, my kicks.
Kick yourselves off my toenails
till that Great Quickstrike
with you, deadstock anew,
tonal gold, the Lord's own grail.

  May the hellhound's marring maw
  snare only air
  as you ascend clear
  of Judgment's concertina barbs.

EULOGY FOR AN AFRO PICK

Don't beat me in the head. —Q-Tip

is over my Dax is over my wax

is over my fried is over my dyed

is over my laid is over brush fade

is over my bob is over my baldy

is over my S is over my curl

is over my Billie is over my Dee

is over my locs my Bantu Knots

is over my corn is over my row

is over my Let's is over my Jam

is over my Just is over For Me

is over my Quo is over my Vadis

is over my Ceaz is over my freeze

is over my Indian over in me

is over my Spanish is over my islands

is over my lye is over my good is over my hair

is over *my goodness!* is over *my God!*

is over *how much?* is over my budget

is over my yaki is over my tracks

is over my crimped is over my trained

is over my mane is over my tail

is over my press is over my whipped

is over my bone is over my strait

is over my dookie is over my plait

is over my micro is over my braid
is over my soul is over my glow
is over my drop is over my drip
is over my teeth is over my fist
is over o please it's over don't be
is over my head is over don't beat
is over my head o please don't be over
it's o not my heat it's over my black
my beautiful black o it's over o head
no over it's over don't o no it's over
my hair no it's over—

THE DRIFTERS AFTER SCHOOL

Ben E. King 4/30/15, Furman Kearney 3/1/17

Once, King's cream and creak throatwork drifted
my mind off eating Jif® with jelly, and I spun.
So yellow I was, I had to know having not: *do I have Soul?*

I had to ask Pops, who'd know, said "son" through gin baleen
then leaned his brown bulk to cello squalls, up for air, breached that deep,
grace to scrape popcorn ceilings. Roof—my mouth's—
I tongued the mush of Wonder®.

> *first you bust the shell, you mash the nut,*
> *you strip the vine, crush concords flat,*
> *you break the bread, then take the knife.* "Son,"

out his head tone. There goes his baby who'd know soon
what whiffs of fun were gin, though fun,
though, still. Feels in tide will drift from rough to clement glass.

When I learn the man has past, my "won't cry,
I won't cry," breaks on a crooner gone to sing alone,
in his mouth an ocean of done tune.

FIRE

GOD we cry because nobody do us like the body—

  O Jesus   love me   this I

  no place low enough

  to keep me   high enough

        for when I feel

         filled with it   I

      am not ashamed to kneel

      not ashamed to sing

    When I have *that name*

in my mouth an *o*

        turned *oh*—An *i*

        turned *a*—I am sangin and

        turnt—What I owe

to the blood what flowed—

        What we *oh* we owe   alive—

that body by that Spirit—

        What's flowing by the Spirit isn't

           ghost lest we ghost it—I eye from

the row in the body of or up in it

        my body up in my robe   my eye roll up to lift

to wonder from where I get

        what come—

        What's ghost isn't spirit   Spirit

         what guide sopranos' keen pierce—Its licked

sweet glow high enough radiating

sweat before me

        what rides high the pierce they make

to go inside us is

    o in this place—Descant shake purl wrung

        what runnels me

        what runs soak altos' shoulder rock

nobody do us

    o Lord—

    Oh the trebled throat on its dark ladder

        what wrassle

come hither   come higher   come lower—

        What wind rattle rock that don't rock

that don't roll—

        What's owed to the body of—

This the blood

       what's shed

come quiver come quaver—Climb lower—

    O go down—

    Oh do I—

Chimes enter tenors—Swayers

           sang now get happy they got it in them—

           get it in me filled with

    what ode   *I know it was*

           I know it was

           I know it was the blood

bear down over it   a clef bowed low enough—

For the tremulous—Tremor   the things of the Spirit—

In this place

the basses   we come   go down   not ashamed—I eye

to come   go down—

O deep Black zenith—GOD

Go down   lift up   take in

what's licked

sweet body of the body of

what's on high—

O   go down—

O[h] O[h] O[h] O[h] O[h] O[h] O[h] O[h] O[h] O[h] O[h] O[h] O[h]

That GOD—

Good Spirit flow pierced run swayed bowed

what we owed the body   I see

we sang

a sweet body of

the sweet body—We give   *I know it was*—

What flow—   In the row

in the body of

the things of the Spirit—

I turn a rock rocked   tremor turnt thing, no body—

I know it was

I know it was

my mouth full of sweat

what chime with

what I know it was supposed to be

but shed like a skin like a robe—

O I went down

to the row in

the sweet body of

                                              I see

                                              I hear

                what's said

                what's said was too ashamed to owe—

                What flowed from the Spirit

                        I know it wasn't

                        I know it wasn't

                what   I see

                            some said—

like a snake

like a shame

                What I owe

                what I owe   when down in the row

                            the Word don't do me—

                What I do

                what I do   now

"... SAY THE SACRED WORDS"

kaa-LĒ-lə

Break the lake's thin shell
      and out you up
to ready steady weight—
      as drupe fruit
of more sweet than that.
Where lake coddles pebbles
      and just(!) there('s): sliver reed
silver to flute through

ē-LĪ-jə

Wait—curlew—of suddenly
      cry abates, purls to—
uh-uh: hunched gust sways
      the gate frame to where thyme lay
though the gate won't shut. You
      drink a little
      here, it's cold. Drink,
      it's good—

ni-KŌL

and then *go*
  not yet though:
yeah cooling thing
  can menthol me (!)till—
 that warm that hot
  round, that teetering
lantern my lit
  tongue cups, still

MANESOLOGY

—after Charlottesville but before it, too, shit

They called me, *say, speak on The Problem,*
they said I could do it from home
where children with books run in circles,
bright riots of color and holler.

       Sure:
I'd speak on The Problem,
since we do, as always been—

Night of it, N and I
misgave it as ours,
making ruck in the rented house,
nicked and dug at *it* that night,
   thus "us"
   as all the while reckoning us
   as tearing at what's ours
until we sat jostled, settled
just as how we "supposed to"—
though what we then chose to
was kiss awhile.
   This looks like wounds
   when your whole skin is your mouth—
   as it must, because what's The Problem

is what we "must" do
we must stay doing's for

      The Problem, I said I *been* saying
      like we must mule some pallid-ass hearts,
      our backs, carts, or our blood a soap
      for shit that's their ashes made ours,
      then be the brain their spectral mulling
      can murmur in like a house
      they call to beck: *speak on The Problem.*

      N said: *that's why the nerves,*
the kind of what she say
is just what I'm saying is

      after working that problem down
      to a faint rattle of chains,
      a vague keen in the walls,
we fucked like a burning church.

      We were shut to it, bones ours,
minds crackling with us
was someone's problem, *their* problem:
their tangled sheetfuls of tantrums—

If I spoke from my home
would I say how we fucked,
drowning knocking and moaning
with moaning, knocking? Phone ringing
like poltergeists wrecking a pantry,

gnawing the fog of their tongues
and their hangnails, so hungry
for skin, for blood, dark skulls to hant.
Always calling and calling,
still ringing and ringing,
we are tired and done
and hold all that we own.

      I answer the phone
      I speak on.

A problem:

night after what happened, the girl clambered into our bed for half the night, after reading about ghosts.

The boy, though, slept, a babe, under blades, fan spinning back to where it started and
                                  back to where
                                        and back to
                                            and

ACKNOWLEDGMENTS

&

NOTES

ACKNOWLEDGMENTS

My thanks to the editors of the following publications in which versions of these poems appeared often under different titles (*):

Best American Poetry 2020 ("Sho"), *Bird Float, Tree Song* ("Livestock"), *boundary 2* ("Buck," "Promissory Note*," "Borax*," "Static*," "Fire*"), *The Iowa Review* ("Property Values" and "First, She Cuts the Stems"), *Lana Turner* ("Negroes Are a Fatsuit, ❤ Hollywood, USA"), *The Los Angeles Review of Books* ("Manesology"), *A Moment of Silence* ("Close"), *The Nervous Breakdown* ("Livestock"), *The New Republic* ("The Drifters After School"), *PEN America* ("Just Wanna Be Like*"), *Ploughshares* ("The Showdown*"), *Poetry* ("... Fox!" and "Sho"), *Public Pool* ("Deformation*"), *Sewanee Review* ("Everyday [I Gets]" and "Black Flight"), *Southampton Review* ("The Post-"), *Virginia Quarterly Review* ("Welter*"), *What Nature* ("Sand Fire [or The Pool, 2016]—"), *Who's in a Name* ("'... say the sacred words'*").

Thank you to the fantastic staff at Wave Books for putting such tremendous care and work into this book. Blyss, Catherine, Heidi, Joshua, and Matthew—thank you!

Thank you to Crisis for setting it down.

Special thanks go to Yona Harvey (genius, gentle instigation, a straight razor, and the Holy Spirit), LaTasha N. Nevada Diggs ("... showing your receipts!" kept me going, sis), Amaud Jamaul Johnson (Big Dogg'ed strength and "KMNOYM"), Evie Shockley (for sound boarding "horde" synonyms even when the poem didn't fit in), Diana Arterian (for nerding passionately on sequence), to Rebecca Wolff (for convincing me to change the title and other encouragements), and always the first: Nicole McJamerson.

I have the fortune of being in conversation with many people about individual poems in this collection. I am grateful to CM Burroughs, Cornelius Eady (dance crazes), Adam Fitzgerald, Cathy Park

Hong, Dawn Lundy Martin, Saretta Morgan, Kate Nuernberger, Bao Phi, Justin Phillip Reed, and TC Tolbert. And to so many friends and peers who have given me encouragement and support along the way. Thank you!

Thank you Elijah and Khalilah (my [de]lights), Ma, my family everywhere, and Dallas: we're all that's left of the O.G. 594. I love all y'all.

Gratitude to the communities of Los Angeles and the Twin Cities, filled with activists, artists, and scholars who have made these places homes with doors open and hard work to do. I've seen smoke over these cities, from sparks natural and systemic. I write this the same week officers of the MPD murdered George Floyd. But the poems in *Sho* have been written over the course of years.

Gratitude to my students from CalArts and the University of Minnesota, Twin Cities, as well as my colleagues on staff and faculty in both schools. Gratitude, also, to my students and student facilitators on "Sharpened Visions."

Thank you for reading these poems, and I hope, many others by many other people.

And like right before a reading when I fix to cuss at the audience: I thank God.

NOTES

In 2016, the Sand Fire blazed from July 22 to August 3, burning more than 41,000 acres of land, primarily in L.A. County's Angeles National Forest.

"Livestock" is a dis•articulation poem, written through a collaborative process with Terry Wolverton.

Mni and pa, as found in "Close," are, if my research was acceptable, Dakota.

"Sho" is a torchon, a form created by Indigo Weller. It incorporates aspects of a sestina; however, teleuton sequence is modified to follow particular variations of lace weaving patterns.

"Just Wanna Be Like" fragments songs and references/alludes to some films and actors. "Alas for You" is from *Godspell* (Stephen Schwartz and John-Michael Tebelak).

"Deformation" fragments a bar from "Birthday Song" by 2 Chainz (ft. Kanye West) and "Rump Shaker" by Wreckx-n-Effect.

The third strophe of "The Showdown" contains quotes from *Uncle Tom's Cabin; or Life Among the Lowly* by Harriet Beecher Stowe. The fourth strophe owes a debt to Osama Alomar's *The Teeth of the Comb*.

The eulogies were written in response to STACKS, a group show curated by the artist Robert Pruitt in Houston. The artists, Jamal Cyrus, Nathaniel Donnett, Autumn Knight, Phillip Pyle II, M'kina Tapscott, and Garry Reece (collectively known then as Art League Houston) were "[looking] at the relationship between cultural tropes and the notion of an authentic black experience." "Eulogy for a Pair of Kicks" uses several sneakerhead terms—*quickstrike, deadstock, tonal,* and *grail*.

Ben E. King was a member of The Drifters, with whom he sang "There Goes My Baby" among many other hits. He co-wrote his solo smash, "Stand by Me," with Jerry Leiber and Mike Stoller.

"Fire" owes a great debt to a formulation of "spirit" articulated in a public conversation I shared with Alexis Pauline Gumbs and Fred Moten, curated by Terrion Williamson at the University of Minnesota, Twin Cities. It quotes/interpolates several traditional songs of worship. Thanks to Yona Harvey for the close looks.

"'. . . say the sacred words'" takes its title from "Ka 'Ba," a poem by Amiri Baraka.

"Manesology" is a term for the study of ghosts and hauntings—rooted in the Latin *manes*.